Congratulations on Your Graduation